The World's Best Aussie Jokes

A.N. Ocker

illustrated by Peter Townsend

ANGUS
& ROBERTSON
PUBLISHERS

ANGUS & ROBERTSON PUBLISHERS

*Unit 4, Eden Park, 31 Waterloo Road,
North Ryde, NSW, Australia 2113, and
16 Golden Square, London W1R 4BN,
United Kingdom*

*First published in Australia by
Angus & Robertson Publishers in 1986
First published in the United Kingdom by
Angus & Robertson (UK) Ltd in 1986
Reprinted 1986 (twice), 1987 (twice)*

Copyright © Angus & Robertson Publishers 1986

*National Library of Australia
Cataloguing-in-publication data.*

The World's best Aussie jokes.

   ISBN 0 207 15311 6.

   1. Wit and humor. I. Ocker. II. Townsend, Peter.
808.88'2

*Typeset in 12 pt Goudy Old Style Bold
Printed in the United Kingdom*

Acknowledgements

A collection of this kind could not be put together without a great deal of collaboration. The compiler and publishers therefore acknowledge with thanks the contributions of Ian Anderson, David Bagster, Paul Bedford, Trevor Best, Barry Chapman, A. J. Crawford, Bettina Cummins, Wendy Dudley, Roz Gatwood, Steve Gillan, John Gunter, Ian Hamilton, Greg Heckendorf, Ann Kinross, G. & L. Lear, Ken Lee, Bob Lidbetter, Douglas Lloyd, Kenny O'Neill, B. Pagey, A. Parkinson, J. Parker, Samuel Proctor, A. Pryde, Alicia Shephard, Ian Scott, Christine Thompson, Richard Vaughan, H. B. Wallis, Bernie Walsh, Ted Whitmee.

Special thanks also to Phillip Adams, whose findings as a result of his search for the Great Australian Joke in the newspaper columns of this country were passed on for inclusion. Also a special acknowledgement of the work of Bill Wannan and Wilbur G. Howcroft, master craftsmen in the recording of Australian humour. Bill Wannan's *Book of Australian Yarns* and Wilbur Howcroft's work, now found in his *Collected Bush Stories and Verses*, were inspirational and occasionally plundered, with permission.

"We're bloody well broke," said one expatriate Aussie to his mate during breakfast at their Earl's Court pad. "And there's only one answer — work. You know, get a job." As the blood slowly returned to his friend's face, he continued, "I'll slip down and get *The Times*."

When he returned he was pointing excitedly to an ad: "Wanted, Footmen (2). Apply Buckingham Palace."

"Two!" he exclaimed. "Made to order for us."

So, giving themselves a bit of a polish up, they went to the Palace to present themselves and their sad story of financial disaster to the Queen's secretary. He was quite impressed, and eventually said, "Well I'll have to see The Lady. She does all the hiring and firing around here. Just wait in the anteroom and I'll see what gives."

After a short waiting time the secretary returned, accompanied by the Queen who stated that, being Aussies, they'd be quite unsuitable. For whilst employed at Buck. Palace they would be required to wear black velvet pantaloons, white stockings and black shoes with silver buckles. When they protested their eminent suitability, the Queen softened her attitude and said: "Well, when we go to Balmoral it will be necessary for you to wear the kilt, and to wear the kilt you must have good, shapely legs."

After a momentary hesitation, and urged by financial necessity, they both dropped their tweeds for the inspection.

"Very good, very good," said HRH approvingly, "now, could I see your testimonials?"

As they were walking out down the long red gravel drive one bloke said to the other in a slightly disgusted tone of voice: "You know, Dick, if the standard of education had been slightly higher in Wagga Wagga we could have got that flamin' job."

The Allied Hatband Makers and Kindred Industries Union official emerged from Trades Hall after a heavy conference with the bosses and delivered the news to his brothers.

"Okay, mates, it's like this — we won most of what we were after: salary increases retrospective to three years, six weeks annual leave, fares to the Gold Coast, a two-hour lunch break, percolated coffee and Twinings tea. Work hours strictly 9 to 5 on Friday."

"What," one of the brothers cried out, "*every* Friday?"

Aussies don't clock in for work...
They sign the Visitors' Book.

An Aussie was driving down the highway when this white blur passed him going very fast. He accelerated to catch it and found it was a chook running down the road at 147 km/h. He was so amazed that he followed it into a farmer's driveway. Curiosity got the better of him, so he went and knocked on the farmer's door and said, "Excuse me, but I just saw a chook running down the highway at 147 km/h."

"Yeah," said the farmer, "that would have to be one of the new chooks we are breeding."

"Well, how come they go so fast?"

"That's 'cos we breed 'em with three legs."

"Three legs! What for?"

"Well, I like a drumstick, the missus, she likes a drumstick and little Tommy, he likes a drumstick too."

"Bloody good idea," says the man, "what do they taste like?"

"Buggered if I know. Never been able to catch one."

Why do Australian men not eat quiche? Because they can't pronounce it.

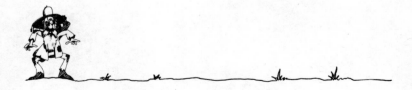

Two boundary riders were out droving sheep during "The Drought", taking a mob from Charleville to the grass "Down South". Quiet sorts of coves, never said much.

They were pushing the mob through Gravesend when they noticed a small shopfront with a sign saying "taxidermist". They got the mob through town and set up camp.

While waiting for the billy to boil, Tim said to his mate, Bob, "Eh Bob, did yer see that shop in town with the sign saying 'taxidermist?'"

"Yeh."

"Wonder what a taxidermist is?"

"Dunno."

"Might ride back into town an' find out while you're cookin' dinner."

"Okay."

So Tim rides back into Gravesend, ties his horse up in front of the shop and wanders in. Of course, the shop is full of stuffed heads of all sorts of animals. The shop owner walks up to Tim and says, "Can I help you?"

"Yeh, I was wondering what a taxidermist does?"

"Well, as you can see, when someone kills an animal we stuff it for them as a trophy."

"Yeh?" said Tim. "I'll be blowed. Tell me, could yer stuff a sheep or a cow?"

"Yes."

"How about an emu or roo?"

"Yes."

With this Tim gets back on his horse and rides back out to camp, dismounts and goes and sits with Bob.

"Well?" says Bob after a long pause. "Did yer find out what a 'taxidermist' is?"

"Yeah," says Tim. "He's just another bloody boundary rider."

The crowd on the Hill were becoming wilder and wilder as the Poms looked set to take the Ashes. As the excitement mounted and beer cans began to fly, one bloke down near the fence started ducking and weaving to avoid the deluge, while a fellow citizen beside him remained calm.

"Don't worry, mate," advised the phlegmatic stranger. "If your name's not on it you're safe. That's what we used to say during the war."

"That's fine for you to say mate," came the worried reply, "but my name's Foster."

An Englishman was on holidays in Australia and decided to take a drive in the countryside. As he passed by a paddock, he noticed a young child desperately fleeing a furious bull which was steadily gaining on her. The Englishman slammed on his brakes, bundled out of his car, vaulted over the two-metre-high paddock fence, and sprinted at amazing speed towards the bull.

Unknown to him, an Australian journalist was passing by and witnessed his incredible feats of courage.

The Englishman had by now reached the bull and, grabbing it by the horns, stopped its charge only five centimetres from the little girl. He flipped the bull over on its back and, twisting its head by the horns, broke its neck.

The Australian journalist was astounded. He ran over to the Englishman and said: "Starve the lizards! That was unbelievable mate! I don't believe I saw it! I've never seen a man with so much strength and courage and daring! It makes me proud to be an Australian! I'll put this story on the front page of my paper! Now, just give me a few details about yourself. Born around here, were you?..."

Next day, the following headline appeared on the front page of the paper: "POMMIE BASTARD KILLS CHILD'S PET!"

There's this swaggie...out back o' Cobar...
40°C in the shade...waterbag empty...

He's been tramping the same featureless plain for four days, passing through large paddocks, each with a gate that must be opened and closed after him. Now, just when the midday heat is building to an intolerable peak, a Range Rover pulls up and the squatter leans out.

"Need a lift there?" he asks.

The swaggie looks at the squatter, at the air-conditioned Rover, the sun, the road ahead and then back to the squatter.

"Nah. Open your own bloody gates."

The stranger at the bar was well dressed and well groomed. He was quietly sipping his first gin and tonic when a sun-bitten, sweat-stained farmer lunged desperately towards the bar, bringing with him the unmistakable odour of sheep.

The stranger watched as he sank four schooners without a pause. "You look done in, sir," he said.

"Done in! I'm bloody rooted mate! I've just finished my shearing and I'm bloody well buggered."

"Well," said the stranger, "I can save you from such exertion in future. I'm from the Shearers and Allied Workers' Association. You just give me the

name of your station, and a few other details, and I'll organise your shearing for you next year. In fact we take care of the whole thing — cooks, musterers, shearers, wool classers, balers, the lot. All that's left for you to do is to cash the cheque from the Wool Board."

"Sounds bloody beaut mate," said the farmer with a huge sigh of relief.

"Right, I'll get the details now." And so saying the shearers' rep took out pad and pencil. "Now, your name and the name of your station."

"Bill Burke of Wogan Creek Station."

"How many hectares?"

"Three hundred and twenty-seven thousand."

"How many sheep?"

"Sixteen."

"Pardon?"

"Sixteen."

The shearers' rep looked at the farmer, who was unconcernedly sipping his sixth schooner. "You mean to tell me you have 327,000 hectares and only 16 sheep?" he asked.

"Yeah."

The shearers' rep closed his sagging bottom jaw, licked his pencil and straightened his notebook.

"What are their names?"

It's during the Depression when, late one evening in a country town, an old swaggie knocks on a lonely door. He hears footsteps approaching and the door opens, revealing a man with his collar back-to-front.

The swaggie says, "Oh, I'm terribly sorry to disturb you, Father."

"I'm not a Father," says the bloke. "I'm a Church of England clergyman."

"Whatever, I'll be on my way."

"No, no. Come on, and tell me what we can do for you."

Unused to religion, the swaggie was a bit shy. "I don't want to come in. I'm goin' around seein' if I can get a meal in return for an odd job or two. I cut wood and stuff like that."

The clergyman says, "You are more than welcome. Sadly, I've just finished cutting our wood. However, if you'd care to stack it at the back of the house I'd be most pleased. And, of course, I'd give you a meal in exchange."

So the swaggie stacks the wood, washes his hands and stands on the verandah at the back of the house. The clergyman insists that he enter, sitting him down at the kitchen table.

There's not much conversation during the meal. At the end of dinner, the swaggie says, "Thanks, Father, I'll be on my way."

"No, no, relax. Be comfortable. You can sleep out on the verandah tonight if you like."

"Thanks very much, but I've got to be getting along."

"Well then, before you go, let me pour you a cup of tea."

The swaggie pours some into his saucer, blows on the surface and drinks it down. Meanwhile, the clergyman has opened his Bible and is having a good read.

The swaggie looks at him curiously and says, "Must be a good book."

The clergyman lifts his eyes and says, "As a matter of fact, it's *the* Good Book."

"Oh yeah . . . What's it about?"

"Surely you know what the Bible's about?"

"Well, I've heard of the Bible."

"You've never read it?"

The swaggie's a bit embarrassed. "Well, you see, I can't read."

"That's nothing to be ashamed of my man. That's why there are people like me involved in the Church. We're able to read the word of God and pass it on to our less fortunate brethren."

"Yeah, well what's it about?"

"Well, it's about quite a number of things. All sorts of stories. Stories of the Flood, of our Saviour. This particular part that I'm reading now is about an extremely powerful man of God.

"He was a man called Samson who came from a little town called Jerusalem. And he had a woman called Delilah. And these particular

verses describe him joining Delilah in the fields while she was grinding the corn. Suddenly they were descended upon by 5000 Philistines. Samson called on God, picked up the jaw bone of an ass, slew 3000 of them and completely routed the rest."

The swaggie looks at the minister in astonishment. "And would this be a true story?"

"Of course it's true. It's the word of God."

"He must have been a pretty strong sort of bloke."

"Oh, an extremely powerful man. As a matter of fact he was capable of tearing down temples with his bare hands. Simply by pushing over the pillars."

"Fair dinkum?"

"How could it be anything else? It is, as I've emphasised, the word of God."

"Yeah, I see."

The following evening, late at night, the swaggie's looking for somewhere to camp and sees in the middle distance the glow of a campfire. He wanders up. Tentatively, observing the protocol of the bush, trying not to come too close.

Beside the campfire is an old rabbiter, brewing up a bunny stew in his four-gallon kero tin. He sees the swaggie standing in the shadows and says, "G'day. Come and get warm and help yourself to the stew."

The swaggie gets into the bunny stew very

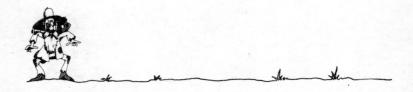

appreciatively and the rabbiter says, "What do you know?"

"Oh, nothing much. Oh yeah, I did hear something. Terrible story. About this big bloke called Simpson. Simpson from Jerilderie. A real bastard. He's going around ripping up the telephone poles. It turns out he was out in the paddock one day giving his girlfriend Delicious a grind in the corn, when all of a sudden 5000 Filipino bastards appeared. So he picks up the arse-bone of a cow, slays 3000 of 'em and completely roots the rest. Turned out to be a bit of a poofter."

One Aussie was so dumb he thought a penal colony was an all-male nudist camp.

How can you tell when an Australian is formally dressed?

He's wearing black thongs.

Then there was the tractor salesman travelling the country back of Bourke. He got talking with a beefy battle-scarred local in the pub and the talk soon touched on football.

"D'ya get to much footy up this way?" the salesman asked the local.

"Hell, yes," came the reply, and with mounting relish the local went on: "Why, just last week we had a great game against the Goanna Gully mob. There was blood everywhere, and skin, hair and beer cans. We had two multiple fractures — broken legs they were — then there were broken noses, smashed-in teeth, an arm or two cracked, as well as most noses. It was flamin' lovely." He paused for a moment to sip his beer. "I heard that one or two of the players got hurt too," he added.

A busload of tourists stops in a remote area of the Northern Territory. The tour guide informs the passengers that just a short distance away there is a cave with some Aboriginal carvings in it. Everybody rushes off the bus to have a look and take photos.

One lady stays on the bus doing her knitting. The guide walks up to her and says, "Excuse me madam, wouldn't you like to have a look at the Aboriginal carvings too?"

"No way!" she says. "I saw a cow calving once, that was enough!"

Comment on the eloquence of the Australian male: "I've seen better conversations in alphabet soup."

A few years back when Australia rode on the sheep's back and wool cheques could be counted on to provide a few meagre luxuries, a squatter arrived in London at the start of his annual continental tour. But, before embarking for Monte Carlo, he paid a call on the Rolls-Royce people to order a new motor car.

They showed him a handsome model priced at £50,000, but he wanted something a little finer.

"This model here is perhaps just what sir has in mind," the salesman purred over an elegant grey model bearing a price tag of £100,000.

No. The squatter had in mind something even better. So they unveiled their latest super, super deluxe model priced at a modest £300,000.

"Yes, this one will do," said the squatter, and began writing out a cheque. "But there's just one thing. Can you install one of those press-button glass windows between the front and back seats?"

The salesman looked a little puzzled, but assured his customer that of course it would be done and would be ready in three weeks.

So in three weeks the squatter returned to take delivery, but the salesman hovered. He was obviously curious and could no longer contain it.

"Sir," he said, "would you mind explaining one thing? We're all extremely interested in your request for the installation of a chauffeur's window. They've been out of fashion for some time now in this country and we didn't think you Australians went in for that sort of thing."

"Ah," said the squatter, "yes, I can understand your puzzlement. I guess none of you have ever had the back of your neck licked by a sheep on the way to market."

Most of their countrymen know of the battle in verse waged by two of Australia's best-loved poets, "Banjo" Paterson and Henry Lawson. Few, however, would know of the somewhat shorter feud conducted by two backblock bards, Ned the Pen and Spinifex Sam. These venerable versifiers died and arrived at the Pearly Gates together. St Peter told them he had only one place, for the better poet of the two. So he tested them by asking for a quatrain ending in the word Timbuctoo. Ned thought for a while and said:

"I gazed across the ocean gray
Where pirates of the deep did lay;
A sailing ship came into view,
Its destination — Timbuctoo."

Sam, quick as a flash, replied:

"Tim and I a-hunting went
And spied three virgins in a tent.
They were many, we were few —
I bucked one, and Tim bucked two."

A jackaroo working on a station in the remotest area of the Territory had one great desire in life — to see the trooping of the colour. Finally he'd saved sufficient to make the trip.

He cleaned himself up, had his first shave for a month, put on the new mail-order suit and hitched to Darwin, in which bustling metropolis he spent a couple of hours in wide-eyed wonderment before boarding the Qantas jet bound for London.

Soon after the steward asked if he'd like anything to drink and read. He ordered a beer, but said he couldn't read.

"Well, you can enjoy the pictures," said the steward, bringing not only an ice-cold tinny but a copy of *Playboy* magazine.

"Good idea," said the jackaroo — and opened the magazine to the centrefold, draped the picture down the seat in front and proceeded to masturbate with great gusto. Having done so, he sat back contentedly and, groping in his top pocket for his cigarettes, he turned to the girl beside him.

"Mind if I smoke?" he enquired.

The races at Birdsville attract many townees to the outback each year. One such arrived after a harrowing drive through the heat and dust. He sank gratefully onto a chair in the local restaurant and it was then that he noticed that the menu was rather peculiar. All that was on it was ham sandwiches, roast pork, pig's feet, bacon and pork chops. Suddenly his appetite deserted him.

"I'll just have a glass of water," he told the waitress.

"I think I ought to warn you," she said, "that we only have bore water."

"Stone the flamin' crows!" he replied, retreating in horror, "you sure don't waste much of that pig!"

Did you hear about the Australian who thought that aperitif was a set of dentures?

* * * * * * * * * *

And then there was the Australian who thought Chou En-lai was Chinese for bed and breakfast.

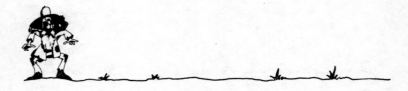

Two mates were out rabbiting, when Harry had to answer Nature's Call. While in the process he let out an almighty scream — he'd been bitten on the penis by a tiger snake!

Quick-thinking Fred laid him down, tied a tourniquet around the affected part, and set out to find a doctor. When he arrived in town he found the G.P. about to perform a delivery, so he politely interrupted. "Excuse me, Doc. My mate Harry's out in the scrub and has been bitten on the prick by a tiger snake; can you come out and treat him?"

"As you can see son, I'm flat out here. You'll have to go back out and save your mate's life yourself."

"How can I?" said Fred.

"Well," said the doctor, "you will have to cut the bite and suck all the venom out or he will die within the hour!"

On Fred's return, Harry, looking pale and weak, asked what the doctor had said.

"I'm sorry mate," said Fred, "but he said you are going to die."

A farmer entered his home-grown vegetables in the local produce shows for years, and finally one year he won the cup, which was presented to him by the mayor. After the presentation the mayor asked privately, "To what do you owe your success with all these fine vegetables?"

"Manure," replied the farmer, "loads and loads of it."

The mayor's wife took the farmer's wife to one side and said, "Can't you get him to call it 'fertiliser'? Manure, you know, sounds awful on vegetables."

"Look," replied the farmer's wife, "I've been twenty years trying to get him to call it 'manure'."

Big Ed was aptly named. He was a giant roly-poly figure who played front row forward for a Sydney league team. But Ed was in trouble. He had to lose weight or he'd be dropped from the side next season.

"Honest, Doc," Ed moaned to his physician. "I've tried every diet under the sun and nothing will shift the weight. What'll I do?"

"Well, I can help you there Ed," the doctor replied. "As a matter of fact I've had great success with this method, but you may not like it."

"Try me Doc," begged Ed.

"Well, Ed, first I must tell you that you can

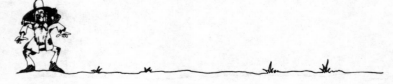

consume anything you like, anything at all and as much of it as you like as well. But you must do so anally."

"What! Bung it up me . . ."

"Exactly so, yes," the doctor interjected.

Ed overcame his shock and agreed to try it. Three weeks later he was back in the surgery — looking slimmer, fitter and very cheerful.

"I feel great. No trouble about me tucker — I just eat anything I like — shove it all in up me . . ."

"Yes, you look good Ed," the doctor rejoined.

Six weeks later Ed checked in again. Kilograms lighter and fighting fit.

"Doc," cried Ed exultantly, "you wouldn't believe it, but just before I came I had a whole pavlova. Just bunged the lot straight up the Khy . . ."

"Well, that's great Ed. But just come and see me once more in another three weeks."

Three weeks later Ed is in the surgery, jiggling up and down on the chair, wriggling round and round. In fact he's incapable of sitting still and finally jumps up and twists and turns around the office.

"Ed, this is dreadful. You've been overdoing it. There shouldn't be this nervous twitching, this hyperactivity . . . I'll have to take you off the diet."

"No, no Doc, it's okay," replied Ed, mid-twist. "I'm just eating a Mintie."

Apart from the lamington, the pavlova and the square meat pie, Australia can boast little by way of local cuisine. To overcome this indigenous dearth, two Australian restaurateurs advertised that their new eatery would supply anything from any cuisine in the world — crêpes, lasagne, paella, chow mein, borsch — whatever a customer wanted, they would provide it or would pay $500 in gold coin to the dissatisfied patron.

The restaurant was flourishing. The all-Aussie staff had mastered the cooking and presentation of the exotic and the ordinary from all parts of the globe. Then one night a customer asked for Tibetan poi.

Calamity, they could not serve it. Worse, they had never heard of it! What was it? They could find it in no known recipe book. The customer received his gold pieces and went to eat elsewhere. The owners decided to investigate the mysterious dish and it was agreed one of them should make the perilous journey to Tibet to learn its secret.

Six months later, having survived a bout of yellow fever in Delhi and a local uprising in Nepal, and narrowly missing inundation by avalanche in the high Himalayas, the restaurateur made it to Tibet and to Lhasa, its capital.

He found the best eating place in town and sat waiting to give his order.

"G'day." The waiter stood pencil and pad in hand. "What'll it be mate?" Yes, he was a fellow

Aussie, working his way to Europe.

"I'll have Tibetan poi, please."

"Yeah, right, but which — apple poi or poi with chips?"

In the bleak hour before dawn the cocky and his brand-new offsider had a couple of boiled eggs and tea for breakfast. Then the farmer said, "Well Jack, s'pose we better get crackin'. Had enough brekker? No? Well . . . p'raps we'll have lunch now. Save comin' all the way back here at midday."

So a couple more eggs and several cups of tea went the way of breakfast.

"Well, now we'd better be off," the cocky said. "Had enough now? What? You'd like some more? Well, tell you what . . . if you'd like to have your supper now, that'd mean we could work on right through the day without interruption."

"Suits me," said the new hand.

So the cocky boiled some more eggs and brewed some more tea. When these had been consumed, he said rather testily: "Right-o, you've had your supper. Now come on, let's get to work!"

"WHAT!" the new hand exclaimed, "WORK — after SUPPER? Cripes, I NEVER work after SUPPER!"

Then there was the station owner who signed on a new hand and sent him out to dig twenty post holes for the home paddock fence.

Later in the day the boss went out to inspect the work and he found the new hand sitting beneath a tree leisurely rolling a cigarette.

"Hey," the boss shouted, "I told you to dig twenty holes and there are only eighteen. What's the idea?"

"Well boss," the newcomer replied, after licking the cigarette paper carefully. "I dug twenty holes. Some bastard must have pinched two."

"Look Shirl, you complain about me and *my* lovemaking," Norm confronted his wife, after a few cold tinnies for courage. "But I've been watching these television couples, and well, you're not so hot either, you know."

"What d'ya mean?" Shirl was stung into asking.

"Well, Shirl, on tele when they're at it, you know, having a naughty, well the woman goes on with a lot of low moaning and stuff. Well, I'd kinda like that from you."

So Shirl agreed to give it a go and the next time they were having a naughty Norm reminded her about the low moaning.

"Righto," Shirl agreed. "I'll begin now . . . Christ Norm, when are ya goin' to finish the bloody kitchen?"

At a Council meeting in a town out west of Bourke a rather snobbish and unpopular Councillor arose and proposed that a bridge be erected over a certain creek. Such a bridge, by the way, would benefit no-one but the very gentleman who recommended the project.

At this, a fellow member jumped up and protested vigorously. Said he: "Put a bloody bridge over a little squib of a creek like that? You must be off your rocker. Why, I could spit halfway across the blasted thing!"

Highly enraged, the first member banged the table and shouted: "You're out of order, sir. Out of order!"

"I know that," bellowed back the dissenting one, "otherwise I'd spit *right* across the bloody thing!"

In Cairns one time, an old digger boarded a train. Rather unsteadily, he seated himself opposite a Salvation Army officer. For some time he studied the officer's uniform with solemn concentration. Finally he spoke. "What's your regiment, Dig? I don't seem to recognise it."

"I'm a soldier of the Lord," replied the other proudly. "I go to Townsville to fight the devil, then to Brisbane to fight him again, and then down to Newcastle, Sydney and Melbourne."

"Thass the stuff, mate," applauded the digger. "Keep on headin' the bastard south."

"You can't change a fiver!" cried the old swaggie. "Bloody beautiful! What sort of a pub is this? What kind of booze artists do you have in this town?"

"The same sort they've got anywhere else," the nettled publican replied defiantly.

"By cripes, they're not. Where I come from men are men. Can't change a fiver! Good heavens! Whoever heard the likes?" And the old bloke cursed derisively into his whiskers.

"Look here, mate," said the publican, "you're slinging off a bit early. Where you come from men may be men, but around here some of them are camels.

"You got a mighty lot o' skite about yer, but can yer beat this — fourteen rums in an hour, done by old Peter the Gouger, and able to walk the chalk line after 'e done it, too?"

The old bloke turned his eyes on the fourteen crosses chalked on the wall. "Of course I can beat it, and the drinks're on you," he said.

"You're on," replied the publican, "but if you lose I keep the fiver."

The swagman agreed, and quaffed four drinks while the publican chalked his score.

"Six," counted the publican.

"And here's seven an' eight," said the old bloke.

"Nine," said the publican.

"Ten," said the swagman. So the tally was kept until the old bloke called thirteen.

"Thirteen?" challenged the publican. "Where'd yer get yer thirteen from? It's twelve yer mean."

"Thirteen, I tell yer! None o' yer monkeyin' with the score."

"It's only twelve," declared the publican heatedly.

"I tell yer I done thirteen," the old chap persisted.

"No bung rules here," shouted the publican. "D'yer think I can't count?"

The swagman put down his glass on the counter and mopped his brow in exasperation.

"Look here, son," he said quietly, "if there's goin' to be any flamin' argument about it, clean yer b—— slate and we'll start from scratch again."

Australian male foreplay — No. 1.
Nudging his sheila in the ribs: "You awake?"

How can you tell when an Australian invalid is getting better?
He tries to blow the froth off his medicine.

Before surfaced roads were introduced, the black-soil plains of Queensland during the wet were sticky enough to give a traveller pause. Not many ventured forth.

It was therefore unusual that McPherson, the squatter, was out and about, picking his way carefully through the mud. Suddenly he spied a familiar hat and, reaching out with his stockwhip, he very carefully lifted it up.

There beneath it was Dan the bullocky, up to his ears in mud.

"Dan," observed McPherson, "you're really in it."

"I'm okay," Dan replied, "but the team's in pretty deep."

In later times the mud can still trouble some intrepid travellers venturing out to little-visited backblock towns. One such was a travelling salesman from Brisbane. He phoned his office to report his situation.

"Are you stuck Tom?" they asked.

"Nope," was Tom's slow reply. "But if I tried to shoot through I might be."

We've all met 'em overseas ... the typical well-behaved, softly spoken and cultured Aussie tourist. Then there's the not-so-typical types, the loud-mouths always complaining about warm beer. It was one of the latter who was holding up the bar in a London pub declaring London to be the arsehole of the universe and its beer as chunderous as horse's piss.

A beautiful young English lass, hearing his sermon, asked him if by chance he was an Australian.

"Bloody oath mate!" he replied.

So she suggested that, as she had some icy cold Fosters in the fridge at home, he would be very welcome to come back with her to her flat. She was extremely partial to the company of bronzed Aussie men, she admitted shyly.

After a few cans of the chilled amber fluid she invited him to join her in a meal — home-baked meat pie. This he enjoyed with lip-smacking relish — and a plastering of tomato sauce.

The beautiful one then suggested that there were other indoor pastimes they could enjoy together. Would he like to come upstairs and see?

The Aussie fell over his feet in his rush to the stairs.

"How'd ya get a pool table up there?" he cried joyfully.

Then there was the Australian who, on returning from a tour in the Holy Land, said to a friend: "You know, it teaches you a lot about the Bible. They took me to see Dan and Beersheba and I found they were two villages. I'd always thought that they were man and wife — like Sodom and Gomorrah."

There was an American sailor in Sydney during the war, and an Aussie was showing him around. They came to the G.P.O.

The American said. "How long did it take to build that, Aussie?"

The reply was, about twelve months. The Yank said it would take six months in the States.

Then he came to another building. "How long did it take to build this?"

"About three months," said the Aussie, trying to foil the American.

"In the States it would take six weeks."

Then they came to the Sydney Harbour Bridge.

"How long did it take to build that, Aussie?"

The Aussie scratched his head and thought for a second. "Gosh, mate. It wasn't there yesterday!"

Did you hear about the Irishmen who built a bridge over the Nullarbor Plain?
They had to pull it down because too many Australians were fishing from it.

The local cricketer was having a hate session about the captain . . .
"He has me fair snouted," he complained. "He always puts me in to bat in the middle of a hat-trick . . ."

Knock, knock.
    Who's there?
Ann.
Ann who?
Ann other Australian wicket falls.

An American firm drilling for oil in northern Australia had its own men as technicians, but employed a few Aussies as labourers.

One of the Australians inadvertently dropped a heavy hammer down the shaft. Further drilling was impossible until it had been removed, and much time, trouble and money were spent in extricating it.

Following this incident the manager assembled all the men around the shaft and called the Aussie forward. He then presented him with the offending hammer and delivered a most sarcastic speech.

"I want you to accept this hammer as a memento," he told the Australian, "and I hope it will always remind you of the trouble and expense you have caused the company through your crass carelessness." He handed over the hammer. "Now," he concluded, "TAKE IT AND GO."

"Does that mean that I'm sacked?" asked the Aussie.

"It sure does," came the emphatic reply.

"Well, this thing's no flamin' use to me, then," responded the labourer — and dropped it neatly down the shaft again!

Norm was driving his small van, with great caution, when he was pulled over by a traffic policeman.

"Don't be worried sir," the officer said, "you haven't broken the law. But tell me, why is it that, every so often, you pull up and race around the back of the van, and thump on the back door?"

"Well, officer, I have three tonnes of budgies in there, and this is only a two tonne van. If they all land at once, they'll break my springs."

Here's a story about a couple of bushies who'd been working in northern Queensland. Given the vicissitudes of rainfall, they'd had to leave their farms and seek casual employment. A bit of fencing, a bit of shearing. Finally, they'd accumulated a few bob and were considering the future.

"What are you going to do now you've got a couple of quid in your pocket?"

"Thought I might go and take a look at Sinney."

"Yeah, I hear Sinney's a bit of all right."

"Well, I reckon it'll be worth taking a look at."

"Yeah, but it's a long way away. What route are you taking?"

"Oh, I thought I'd take the missus. After all, she stuck with me through the drought."

In the backblocks of Booligal some years back there lived a rather extraordinary old character called Cal. Despite the fact that Cal habitually wore thick, bull's-eye type glasses, he claimed to be a champion with the shotgun. He was also noted for his lack of modesty in describing the marvellous talking powers of his pet cockatoo.

One day Cal arrived at his favourite hostelry with the sad news that the bird had cleared out. His mates plied him with strong drink and commiseration, but the old chap appeared inconsolable. However, the next evening he returned with the joyful news of his pet's recapture.

He explained that while out shooting he heard a rapping kind of sound coming from a nearby box tree. He aimed his trusty gun in that direction, whereupon his cocky thrust its head from out the leaves and called in agitation: "For gorsake don't shoot, Cal! I'll come home."

"But what was the rapping noise you heard, Cal?" asked one of his listeners.

"Well, you see," bragged the old fellow, "that there bird of mine knows what a dead shot I am. As soon as he saw my gun his knees started knocking together — and that gave the game away."

"She's a tough country where I come from, boys," declared a weather-seamed stranger in a bush shanty. "The ground's so stony we have to blast the seed in among the rocks with shotguns and harvest it with ruddy search warrants."

A traveller stopped at a very small township for petrol and found the place deserted. Then he spotted a funeral procession with a very large man and a very large dog in pride of place behind the hearse. Behind them a single file of about a dozen blokes followed in respectful silence.

"Somebody important died?" he asked.

"Yeah, the wife," answered the big bloke.

"What happened?"

"The dog savaged her."

After some thought, the traveller asked, "Do you want to sell the dog?"

"Yeah," said the big bloke, "join the queue, mate!"

Fresh from a rather select school where much value was placed upon good manners and sportsmanship, a young, newly appointed football coach was horrified at the rough and ready style of play adopted by his unpolished, back-country charges.

Determined to bring some system and refinement into their game, he assembled the team for a lecture. He began by saying it was important they learn the correct way to tackle an opponent and prevent him getting off with the ball.

At this, a wild-eyed, battle-scarred ruckman arose and called excitedly: "I know twelve ways, Coach, twelve bloody ways!"

Ignoring him, the coach continued: "The regular method is to grasp the opposing player firmly, but fairly, around the waist causing him to drop . . ." But he was again interrupted by the bushwhacker: "I know thirteen ways, Coach, thirteen bloody ways!"

Have you heard the one about the Aussie punter who lost $100 on the Melbourne Cup and $500 on the replay?

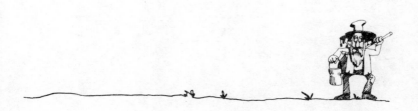

There is this story about the punter who'd spent a little too long at the bar. He noticed a sign that read: "Lunch 12 to 1." Not bad odds, he thought as he caught the barman's eye. "'Scuse me, I wanna putsch a bet on lunch."

"You're drunk!" the barman said, "now go home before I throw you out."

So the drunken punter staggered out and down the street. Not far away was another pub where our friend saw a sign saying: "Lunch 11 to 2." "The odds are down already!" the drunk thought, "I better hurry up and place a bet." So he went into the public bar, walked up to the barman and requested, "I wanna back lunch at 11 to 2."

"You're drunk!" the barman exclaimed, and threw the punter out.

Well, the punter continued staggering down the road, until he came to the next pub, where there was a sign which read: "Lunch 1 to 2." "That's no good," he thought, "odds on. Well, I may as well go in and see how the race finishes."

Just as he walks in the door the barman shouts out to the cook, "Sausages — one."

"Oh well," our punter said, "just as well I hadn't backed lunch."

Portion of conversation emerging above the din in a country pub:

"What, *him* a chef? Blimey, he couldn't hold a job cookin' at a lost dogs' home!"

Out back of Dunedoo they are a tough breed, but there's none so tough as old Bluey. Bluey could whip the socks off all the younger blokes at work. And at play, he could pop the pants off any rival — drinking, snooker, golf — you name it, Bluey excelled.

One day one of the younger chaps, who'd just lost to Bluey in an armwrestling contest, thought to flatter him and thus find out the secret of his success.

"Bluey, you're bloody amazing. You're good at every bloody thing," he said.

"No, no son. Mind you, I used to be. But now, well, I'm not so good in the old sack any more. The wife Mabel and I now sleep in separate beds and, well, take for example the other night. I felt the old urge come upon me and I called over to Mabel to see if she was willing for a bit of fun that night, and Mabel said that of course she was willing for more fun.

"'More fun?' I asked her.

"'Yes, you were here ten minutes ago,' she said.

"Well, I tell you son — I'm fine but the bloody memory's goin'."

Then there was the Aussie hunter. One day he came across a beautiful young woman who was sunbathing nude on a rock. He took one look at her and asked: "Are you game?"

"Sure am, big boy," she replied.

So he shot her.

Wycheproof, Victoria, has a train line running through the main part of town, which fact rarely disturbs its citizens . . .

The meeting in the town hall had reached the red hot stage. Charges and countercharges were flying around the room when suddenly the front door opened and a man dressed in overalls stepped in. "A minibus is parked on the railroad tracks in front of the town hall," he shouted. "I'm the conductor and want to ask that it be moved."

"I so move," cried a voice from the back of the room.

"I second it," another voice said.

The chairman banged his gavel and said, "You've heard the motion. All in favour say aye."

"Aye," came the resounding cry.

"So ordered," the chairman said. "Now, let's get on with the other business that we were talking about."

Max Brown, a young father-to-be, was waiting anxiously outside the maternity ward where his wife was producing their first baby. As he paced the floor, a nurse popped her head round the door.

"You've a little boy Mr Brown," she said, "but we think you'd better go and have a cup of coffee because there might be another."

Max turned a little pale and left. Some time later he rang the hospital and was told he was the father of twins.

"But," the nurse went on, "we are sure there's another on the way. Ring back again in a little while."

At that, Max decided that coffee was not nearly strong enough. He ordered a few beers and rang the hospital again, only to be told a third baby had arrived and a fourth was imminent.

White-faced, he stumbled to the bar and ordered a double scotch. Twenty minutes later he tried the phone again, but was in such a state that he dialled a wrong number and got the recorded cricket score.

When they picked him up off the floor of the phone box the recording was still going strong.

"The score is 96 all out," came the voice from the other end, "and the last one was a duck."

A visitor walked into the Ettamoga Hotel.

"Long time since I've seen sawdust on the floor of a pub."

"That's not sawdust, it's yesterday's furniture after the white ants got it."

Then there was Bazza who walked into a pub in north Queensland leading a giant freshwater crocodile on a leash.

"Do you serve Pommies in this hotel?" he enquired.

"Yes, sir. We serve English people."

"Good, I'll have a beer for myself and a couple of Pommies for the croc."

An Irishman went for a job interview and was told he would have to pass an IQ test in order to qualify for it.

"Sure, an' what's an IQ?" asked the Irishman.

"Well," said the employer, "if a person has an IQ of 170 he could go to university; but a person with an IQ of 70 might have trouble tying his shoelaces."

"Ah," said the Irishman, "so *that's* why so many Australians wear thongs!"

There was this guy from Gulargambone who hurried into the confessional and breathlessly recounted his sin.

"Father, I made love to me wife."

The priest explained that, far from being a sin, lovemaking between married couples was condoned by the Holy Church.

"But Father, I made love to her with lust."

Again the priest reassured him that, while the Holy Church recommended avoiding overly excessive carnality, a little lust between husband and wife was not a sin.

"But Father, I made love to her with lust when she wasn't expecting it. There she was, bending over the deep freeze to get out a frozen chook when suddenly I felt the urge to have her — and I did."

By this time the priest was a little fed up with what seemed to him like skiting, so he suggested the bloke say three Hail Marys and attend church more often.

"What," cried the sinner. "Don't I get banned from church?"

"No, why?" asked the priest.

"Well, I've been banned from Woolies."

Have you heard about the Irishman who emigrated to Australia and raised the IQ in both countries?

"Is that the train for Wagga pulling out?" the young jackaroo cried as he dashed to the barrier at Central Station.

"Either that or the station's backing up," grinned the guard.

Then there is the tale about the coach from the city who was engaged to tutor a newly formed team in the backblocks. Fresh from the "big time", he taught the lads all the tricks of the trade. To his dismay, however, his team was badly beaten in each of the first five matches they played.

Disgustedly, he called the players together and, in a bitter diatribe, told them they were, without doubt, the biggest bunch of morons and no-hopers this side of the rabbit-proof fence.

"And now," he concluded, "I'm going to start teaching you galoots all over again — right from the beginning! Now this object here," he said sarcastically, "is what is known as a football. The idea is for the player to gain possession of it, and . . ."

But he was interrupted by a horny-handed son of the soil who called out pleadingly, "'Old on a bit, Coach — don't go so flamin' fast!"

Not long after the First Fleet had arrived with convicts in Sydney Cove, the British Government sent out a senior ranking officer to look over the colony. The next day, Monday, being a public holiday (yes, we Australians invented the long weekend) the commandant of the garrison, wishing to impress, suggested a sail on the harbour. Unfortunately the wind was light, so a long-boat was laid on with twenty convicts, ten-a-side, with a plank walkway along the centre for the mate to move up and down as he urged on the reluctant rowers with his whip. Great pace was being made, when, suddenly, the rowers fell silent. The mate, sizing up the situation, immediately informed the commandant that one of the convicts had died. Hearing this, the commandant gave his order, whereupon the mate walked up and down whipping the remaining convicts unmercifully; then gave the order:

"Convicts, all on your back, penis out, urinate."

On witnessing this, the home officer exclaimed, "How quaint!"

"Oh no," replied the commandant, "it's an old Australian custom: when a member of the team dies, we always have a quick whip around and a piss-up."

The Hill End council had convened to consider expenditure on a urinal for the town. One of the members didn't know what a urinal was and it had to be explained to him. Whereupon he waxed enthusiastic and demanded that twice the sum asked for should be released. As he explained: "If we're gunna have a urinal we may as well go the whole hog and build an arsenal as well."

What's the difference between a Pommie football team and a 747?
The 747 stops whining when it gets to Sydney.

And while we're having a dig at the Poms, what about the Kiwis . . . How do you set up a New Zealander in a small business?
Buy him a big business and wait.

Two drovers were arguing in the pub one day about the superior abilities of their respective sheep dogs. Said the first drover: "My dog's so smart I can give him half a dozen instructions at once and he'll carry them all out one by one."

"That's nothing," replied the other drover, "I give my Bluey just one instruction and he anticipates the rest."

After a few more beers they agreed to put their dogs to the test. The first drover whistled his dog and told him to run down to the bus stop, turn left and follow the track to the third gate, then go to the fourth paddock and bring back the sheep with the black marking over one eye. With that the dog bolted down the road and out of sight after turning left at the bus stop. Ten minutes later he was chasing the sheep with the black marking over one eye down the main street to the pub.

"Not bad," said the second drover, "now watch this," and he called over his Bluey.

"Bluey," he said, "I'm hungry." And with that Bluey charged off down the road until he spotted a chicken shed. After tunnelling under the fence he found a hen on her nest, pushed her off, grabbed an egg and ran back to his master, dropping the egg at his feet. He then jumped into the back of the ute, grabbed a billy, raced it down to the river and filled it up with water. He put the billy on the small fire that was burning behind the pub, ran back to his master, grabbed the egg and dropped it into the billy. After exactly three

minutes he grabbed the egg out of the billy, raced it over to his master and then stood on his head.

"That's bloody fantastic!" said the first drover. "But tell me — why is he standing on his head?"

"Well, I told you he was smart. He knows I haven't got an egg cup!"

On his first day in his new job, George came across something he couldn't understand. So he asked the man next to him, "Can you tell me, what's a cubic foot?"

"Dunno," said the man, scratching his head, "never heard of it. Ask Ted, the shop steward, he knows everything."

So George went over and asked Ted.

"Cubic foot? Dunno," said Ted. "But I tell you this mate — we'll make sure you get the right compo for it."

If a paddock full of Irishmen is called a "paddy field", what is a paddock full of Australian men called?

A vacant lot.

The banana farmer from Woolgoolga was a smiling, slow-speaking lad, and opposite him on the train north sat a sleek Sydneysider making comfortable passage to the family retreat on Queensland's Gold Coast. But they became acquainted, as strangers do on trains, and soon after the Sydney man said: "You say you are just a banana farmer, but I'm impressed with your general intelligence and commonsense. To pass the time I suggest we play a little game."

"Well, what's your game?"

"I suggest we each ask the other a question, and if we can't answer the other fellow's question we give him a dollar."

"Yeah, that might be a good game. But I don't think the terms are fair."

"What's wrong with the terms?"

"Well, you're a city bloke, you're probably well educated and well travelled. I'm just a poor farmer — only went through to high school, and spent all the rest of my life on the farm. So I suggest that if you can't answer *my* question you give *me* a dollar, but if I can't answer *your* question I give *you* fifty cents."

"That seems fair enough. Let's play. You ask the first question."

"Well, I'd like to know what it is that has three legs and flies."

After some thought the city man said, "Damned if I know. Here's your dollar."

"All right," said the Woolgoolga man, "what's

your question?"

"I'd like to know *what it is* that has three legs and flies."

"Damned if I know. Here's your fifty cents."

What's the difference between an Australian wedding and an Australian funeral? One less drunk!

An ex-station manager once came upon an old-timer who had been camped at the same waterhole for many, many months. As the boss rode up he observed the old man with one of his boots glued to his ear and listening with intense concentration. He glanced briefly up at the rider, motioned him to be silent, and continued listening.

"What's going on?" demanded the boss.

"Listenin' to the Test match," grunted the old-timer irritably.

"Here, let me have a go," said the boss, and held it to his own ear. "Can't hear a thing," he declared.

The old man snatched it back, listened, then shook his head and said: "You're right, dammit. Must be their tea break."

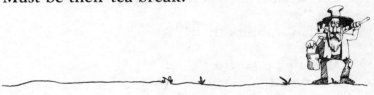

One of the oldest Aussie jokes is about the two swaggies who'd travelled together for many a month and over many a mile. One morning, just past dawn, when the sky was the soft colour of clotted cream and the air crisp and clean, they saw a large black object some distance off. It was obviously dead and decaying so they gave it a wide berth.

About lunch time, the sun hot and high in a bright-blue sky, Bill unclamped his pipe from his jaws and spoke.

"Did you see that dead 'orse?"

It was evening and the first stars were appearing when Bert answered.

"That weren't no 'orse, it were a cow."

The next morning Bert awoke to find no sign of Bill but a scrap of dirty paper. It bore a scribbled note.

"I'm off," it read. "There's too much bloody argument in this here camp."

By comparison Sam and Slim were bloody talkative.

They were making camp one night near the Murray and Sam went to fill the billy while Slim made up the fire. Sam returned and after several minutes spent rolling a cigarette he said, "There's a chap down there."

"Oh," said Bill, "gettin' fish is he?"

"No."

"Gettin' rabbits then?"

"No."

"What's he gettin'?"

"Drowned."

Some famous Aussie names:
Gunner: Nothing to do with the A.I.F. He's gunner get round to it one day.
Wombat: Typical ocker. He eats roots and leaves.
Koala: Likes to climb into the fork at night.

The stewards at an outback racetrack had long suspected a certain owner of giving his horse dope. One day, just before the main race, the chief steward noticed the suspected one making his way surreptitiously to the stables.

Watching closely, the steward saw him slip something into the horse's mouth. "Got you at last!" cried the steward as he grabbed the owner. "You'll get rubbed out for life over this."

Thinking quickly, the owner replied: "Why, these are only homemade sweets the wife makes — look, I'll show you!" He thereupon ate one himself. "Here, you try one," he said, and gave one to the steward who, confused by the turn of events, ate it.

The owner then led the horse to the saddling paddock. "Get in front from the start and stay there," he told the jockey.

"Why so?" asked the jockey. "Is anything likely to pass me?"

Replied the owner grimly: "Just me and the chief stipendiary steward!"

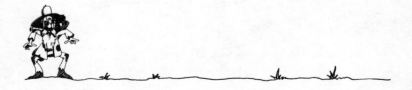

Did you hear about the Aussie accountant who thought Moby Dick was a venereal disease?

An elderly cocky and his son lived for many years just scratching a living from their poor, broken-down farm. One day the son drew a lucky number in a lottery and won $20,000. Overjoyed, he picked out a dollar coin and handed it to his father.

The old chap gazed at it for some time and then said drily: "I hope, son, you won't go throwing the rest of your money away like this. When I was young," he continued, "I was always very careful. I never drank or gambled, and I was especially wary of women. As a matter of fact I never ever married."

"Well, that's lovely, that is!" protested the son. "You know what that makes me, don't you?"

"Yes," replied the father, "and you're a greedy one, too!"

Why did the galah wear a raincoat? He was polyunsaturated.

All of the gang working at the grape harvest agreed that "Big Robbo" was a skite and a blow-hard. Nonetheless, they were forced to admit he was a pretty tough hombre, for all that.

The mosquitoes that year were about as big as hornets and twice as ferocious. When they started their bloodthirsty cacophony of hate around sundown the noise was like a hundred dentists' drills — only more intimidating.

Big Robbo, however, seemed virtually impervious to their most pernicious onslaughts, and boasted accordingly. Finally, the big fellow bet good money he could endure being tied stark naked in some thick scrub behind the camp for a full hour after nightfall. Most of the gang hastened to cover the bet, as the mossies were known to be particularly fierce in that locality.

Next evening Robbo was escorted into the mulga, stripped to the buff, and left with his hands tied firmly behind his back around a stout sapling. The rest hurried back and sat huddled round the cow-dung fires.

Time passed, until a half hour had ticked away. Suddenly, terrifying screams, oaths and piteous cries for help rent their ears. Racing back, they released the distressed man and assisted him back to camp, where be flopped into his bunk and covered himself with blankets.

"So, the old mossies were more vicious than you thought, eh Robbo?" one of the men remarked with quiet triumph.

Robbo raised himself on one elbow and glared balefully at the speaker. "Mossies — nothin'," he snarled savagely. "I'd 'ave been right as rain if the blockies round 'ere only 'ad the sense ter keep their bloody poddy calves tied up at nights!"

A well-known local identity from Gulargambone was a marvellous speller, cross-worker, boggle player ... but he used to spell very slowly and deliberately. He entered the national spelling championship but was defeated in the finals. His explanation afterwards to his mate was: "Buggered if I knew that A-U-S-P-I-C-E spelt "Orsepiss'."

A tractor salesman from Gunnedah tells the story of approaching a wheat farmer to sell him a new tractor, only to find him resting on his verandah patting his pet dog. Only on closer examination it turned out to be a pig with a wooden leg.

As much to put off the inevitable wheeling and dealing about the price of the tractor as anything, the salesman remarked that the pig had a wooden leg. "Some pig that," replied the cocky, "saved my missus." He went on to recount a story where two scoundrels had come to the house whilst he was away, with the intention of robbing it. The pig had sent them packing.

"But it's got a wooden leg," said the salesman.

"Quite a pig," said the cocky. "Saved my kids from drowning." He went on to explain that the kids had been playing in the dam and got into difficulties. Whereupon the pig launched himself into the water and pushed them to safety.

"But it's a wooden leg, isn't it?" said our intrepid salesman.

"A bonzer pig, this is. I remember once when the kerosene fridge caught alight. We would have all been burnt to death in our beds if it wasn't for that pig."

And he gave it a fond pat.

"But I'm still interested in how come it's got a wooden leg," said our salesman.

A sentimental smile spread over the cocky's face. "Well, if you had a pig as good as this, would you eat him all at once?"

An English chap fell in love with an Irish lass. Even after being welcomed into her parents' home he felt a little peculiar, as if he were somehow different. Finally he went to the doctor to see if there were tablets or exercises or anything that would help him fit the scene, to help him act more Irish.

The doctor suggested an operation to remove ten per cent of his brain. This, he assured him, would make the average Pom similar to the average Irishman. Being madly in love he went into the hospital and had the job done.

He awoke to find an obviously agitated surgeon pacing up and down the room. Seeing him stirring, the surgeon said, "Look, before you say anything, there is something you should know. We've had a terrible week here. Changing staff. Big influx of patients. Last-minute change of theatre. And the long and the short of it is that instead of taking ten per cent and leaving ninety per cent we've made a mess and taken ninety. Now you've only ten per cent. So that's it. What have you got to say?"

"No worries Doc. She'll be right mate."

A man walks into a pub and asks for a middy and two small liqueur glasses full of beer. The barman is curious as to why he wants such small glasses of beer, so he follows him out to his car where the man gives the glasses to two little blokes in the back. These little blokes are only about twelve inches high. The barman is so astonished he asks, "How come they are so small? I have never seen anyone that little. What are they — leprechauns or somethin'?"

"No," says the man. "They're just a couple of Australians with all the bullshit knocked out of 'em."

A ustralian male foreplay — No. 2.
"Brace yourself, Raelene."

W hy do Australian men come so quickly?
So they can get to the pub and tell their mates about it.

The afternoon air was rich with the sounds of the radio commentator's voice calling the races.

"Harry," shouted the deafened wife, "turn that thing down. Think of someone else for a change. I swear all you ever think about is horses."

"Eh?" responded her spouse.

"Well, it's true. I bet you care more about horses than you do about me. You've probably even forgotten the day you asked me to marry you."

"Nah, Shirleen luv, I remember that. It was the day they had to shoot poor old Tourmaline's Pride after the Bankstown Welter at Rosehill."

Why wasn't Christ born in Australia?
Well, where would you find a virgin or three wise men?

What do you get when you cross a kangaroo with an elephant?
Bloody big holes all over Australia.

A young executive is desperately trying to impress a business associate in an expensive restaurant. On the way to the gent's he spots Rupert Murdoch at a corner table and fawns all over him. Mr Murdoch is his hero, his guiding star. Would there be any chance at all of Mr Murdoch passing by his table and impressing the business associate by saying, "Hello David"? Is that too much to ask?

In due course Rupert Murdoch obliges, only to have the young man look up and snarl, "Piss off Rupert, can't you see I'm busy?"

"Hey mate, what ya doing?" the nosy on-looker enquired of the nearest workman. There were three of them, digging out a fair-sized hole at the edge of Lavender Bay, Sydney.

"Haven't you heard?" The foreman looked up and wiped his brow. "It's finally happening . . . we're starting to dig the tunnel under the harbour."

"Gees, really? How long will it take?"

"Well, with sickies, annual holidays, long-service leave, funerals to attend and strikes . . . we estimate we'll be finished in about fifteen years."

"Gees, that long eh?"

"Yeah. If I was you I wouldn't wait. Take the ferry."

Work! In Australia most people stop looking for work the moment they find a job.

Why do Australian men make love with their eyes closed?
Because they can't stand to see women enjoying themselves.

Aussie etiquette:
"Got a match, Tom?"
"No, but I got a lighter."
"How'm I gonna pick my teeth with a lighter?"

How does an Aussie woman gain her man's attention?
She drops her handkerchief . . . after wrapping it around a can of beer.

Dave was a wharfie who had the security guard thoroughly puzzled. Every day when he left the Port Melbourne docks he wheeled out a wheelbarrow full of rubbish, and every day the guard would sift through the rubbish, certain that Dave was pilfering.

Dave had that look in his eye — and a superior grin. It was infuriating because every day the guard found nothing but rubbish.

When Dave retired, the guard couldn't bear to let him go without knowing.

"Dave, I know you were pilfering but I don't know how. What was the secret? What were you stealing?"

As he headed through the gates and towards a new life at Noosa, Dan revealed all.

"Wheelbarrows," he said.

You have to sympathise with the South Geraldton road-building gang. One morning they went out to work and forgot to take their shovels. They phoned the foreman to ask advice.

"Don't panic," he said. "I'll send a van out with the shovels but you'll have to lean on each other till they get there."

"Sid, I'm pregnant," Shirley reported to her boyfriend, "and if you can do nothing to help me I'm going to throw myself off the Harbour Bridge."

"Gees, Shirl, you're great," Sid said with relief. "I mean, not only are you a great screw but you're a good sport as well."

Sam's parents were horrified. Their four-year-old was just learning to talk fluently, which was charming, but he used the great Australian adjective in almost every sentence he uttered, which was less than polite.

They tried every strategy to get him to stop, but nothing seemed to work. So they tried bribery. He could go to Janet's birthday party if he stopped. His father warned Sam that he'd asked Janet's mum to send him home at once if she heard the filthy, disgusting word just once.

On Saturday at 2.30, Sam set off. At 2.50 he was back again in tears.

"I told you not to use that disgusting word," his father railed.

"I didn't use the bloody word. The bloody party's not till next bloody Saturday."

Australian male foreplay — No. 3.
"Make yer a cuppa after?"

To the average Australian there is only one evil worse than drink and that's thirst.

How do you tell a well-balanced Aussie? He's got a chip on both shoulders.

The Red Cross Blood Bank lecturer was visiting a little town in Western Australia. "Of course," he said to the small audience, at the local hall, "you all know what a corpuscle is."

"Most of us do," the chairman interposed, "but you'd better explain for the sake of those who haven't been inside one."

The two young men were in heated discussion, each arguing that their favourite brand of beer was the best in the world.

Finally the barman suggested they settle the dispute by calling on experts. So samples of each beer were sent to the C.S.I.R.O.

"Gentlemen," the letter of reply began, "we regret to inform you that in our opinion neither of your horses will ever race again."

Why do Australian men piss in the bushes at parties?

Because there's always someone chundering in the toilet.

A wounded G.I. came to in an Australian field hospital and with typical Yankee pathos murmured to the Aussie nurse bending over him, "Did I come here to die?"

"No luv, yer cime here yesterdie," she reassured him.

Question: How do you get an Aussie on a roof?
Answer: Tell him that drinks are on the house.

The Japanese have invented a camera that is so fast that it will actually take a picture of an Aussie with his mouth shut.

Notice outside a church in Hawthorn.
"What would you do if God came to Hawthorn?"
Scrawled in graffiti underneath:
"Make Him full forward."

What does a Double Bay widow wear to her husband's funeral?
A black tennis dress.

The Yank was skiting about the tallest building in the U.S.

"It's so high, the top storey has to be tipped each time a jet flies over," he boasted.

A scornful Aussie quietly drawled, "Well mate, we have one so tall that when a mother accidentally dropped her baby from the top, he walked into the old-age pension office when he reached the ground!"

On her last official visit to Australia, the Queen launched a new ship at Newcastle dockyard and afterwards expressed the desire to meet some of the shipyard staff.

"And this, Your Majesty, is Bob Bunyan," said the escorting official, introducing a massive chap in grimed overalls. "Bob is supposed to be one of the strongest men on the waterfront. Tell Her Majesty how much you can lift, Bob."

Bob shuffled his feet and said modestly, "Oh, about a bloody ton."

"Come off it, break it down," said the shocked official.

"Well, about half a bloody ton," said Bob.

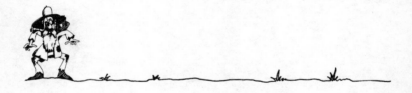

A definition of optimism.
   Kim Hughes going in to bat with zinc cream on his nose.

Things were so tough during the recent dry spell, the council had to close two lanes at the local swimming pool.

Archaeologists in the Northern Territory unearthed a skeleton which they announced with great excitement to be a genuine *Australopithecus*. But of course there were an equal number of experts who disputed the issue. So to settle the debate the skeleton was sent to Canberra for further tests and investigation.

A few weeks later the chief investigator called a press conference to announce the findings. It was definitely *Australopithecus*.

The press asked how he could be so sure.

"We sent it over to the ASIO labs and after two weeks with them, it confessed."

It was a time of great drought when feed had run out on most properties and stockmen took to the public highways to feed large flocks on roadside vegetation.

A Tasmanian local ran into one such flock just five kilometres outside Launceston and he stopped for a chat with the drover.

"Where ya from mate?" he asked.

"Up Coonabarabran way," came the drawled reply.

"Strewth, how did ya get that flock across Bass Strait?"

"Oh, I didn't come *that* way."

And speaking of drought. There was this American touring Australia who landed one night in a little town back o' Bourke. Before setting up his tent he called at the town's only cafe for a meal. Getting up to go he asked the owner, "Do you think it will rain?"

"Hope so," said the owner, peering up at the sky. "Not so much for my own sake as for the boy's. I've seen it rain."

Every year the neighbouring stations of Tambawarrah Downs and Tidbinbilly Plains mustered enough hands to have a game of cricket.

This year Tambawarrah Downs had managed to include a giant on their team. He was a shearer's cook named Tiny who towered above the rest of the men and whose girth was almost as excessive as his height.

Tiny was in and batting and Slim, the slick fast-bowling foreman from Tidbinbilly, had thrice appealed for obvious l.b.w. decisions.

"Not out," the umpire had responded to each.

The next delivery the ball was clearly heard to clip the bat and the keeper came up with the ball in his gloves.

"Howzat?"

"Not out."

"What kind of ratbag decision is that, mate!" Slim exploded. "It bloody well hit the bat. Why don't ya bloody well give him 'out'?"

"Look, sport, I can't do that," the umpire admitted. "We've only got a nine-gallon keg in the truck and Tiny is the best bloody drinker from here to Emu Plains."

What's the definition of an Aussie poofter? A guy that prefers girls to beer.

There are people who swear they were there in court at the time and others who say they knew the prosecutor personally, but the story of the Denenbandy rapist has achieved the status of legend.

He was a young lad, up before the circuit judge and accused of sexually assaulting a local miss. He stood before the defence counsel looking dazed and somewhat puzzled by the proceedings, but answering all questions.

Yes, he'd stopped the car about five kilometres out of Denenbandy.

Yes, he'd persuaded the girl to get out of the car.

Yes, he'd taken his pants off.

"But wait," cried the defence counsel. His case rested on the fact that the plaintiff had not only been willing but provocative. "Wait," he continued, "what was the girl doing all this time?"

"Oh, she was just lying on the rug."

"And how did that make you feel?"

"Well, pretty good really."

"No, I mean did you feel any physiological response to this?"

"Eh?" The youth looked up in puzzled incomprehension.

"Your penis, was it tumescent?" his counsel asked, striving for decorum.

"Eh?" the lad remained blank with puzzlement.

"Were you aroused, man?"

Again the question was met with a blank-faced frown.

"You'll have to speak plainer that that," the judge intervened. "Here, let me try. Your prick, son," he said, addressing the plaintiff, "which way was it pointing?"

"Oh, back to Denenbandy, Your Honour."

It was probably at Denenbandy again that Mick Hogan stood before judge and jury charged with stealing cattle.

The local jury debated for ten minutes after hearing the evidence and found him not guilty. "So long as he returned the cattle."

The judge, infuriated with that finding, blusteringly demanded that they rethink their verdict.

"Not guilty," they declared after two minutes' debate, "and he can keep the bloody cattle."

Why do Queenslanders call their beer XXXX? Because they can't spell beer.

"How far is it to Wagga, mate — as the crow flies?" a traveller outback asked a local farmer.

"Damned if I know sport. The flamin' crows never bloody well leave here!"

The A.B.C. weather reporter was announcing the day's temperature forecasts around Australia. "Perth, 21, Alice Springs, 32, Darwin, 34, Brisbane, 26, Sydney, 22, Adelaide, 23, Melbourne, closed."

The colonel was inspecting his men and, as most were new recruits, the inspection was less formal than usual. He stopped to get acquainted with a few of the newcomers.

Curly was one such newcomer who was looking a trifle uncomfortable when the colonel stopped before him.

"Aren't you happy, man?" he asked.

Curly reluctantly agreed he was rather happy.

"Well come on man, what were you in civilian life?" continued the colonel.

"A bloody sight happier still," said Curly.

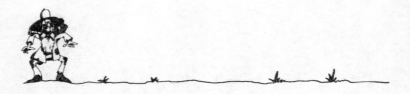

And talking about new recruits . . .

There's the story of Dave who in his mid-thirties planned to enlist in the army. When Ma heard the news she asked Dad to speak to him, so Dad took his son out behind the woodshed to lecture him.

"Listen Dave," he began, "you must be careful of the demon drink. Liquor can do strange things to a man, you know."

"Don't worry, Dad," said Dave. "I've never touched the stuff and I never will."

"Well Dave, there's another thing I should warn you of if you're intent on leaving home, and that's gambling."

"No need to worry, Dad," Dave assured him. "I've never bet a penny in me life and never will."

Dad pressed on bravely with the lecture. By now he'd reached the delicate part of his message.

"Dave, I have to warn you about women, son. Women can be the very devil."

"Say no more, Dad," Dave interrupted. "That's one thing I never do — go out with women!"

Dad returned to Ma with the news.

"No need to worry, Ma. The army won't take that boy. He's a bloody half-wit."

You can tell a South Australian. But you can't tell him much.

The further inland you go the slower Australians speak.

Barney was from way out back of the black stump and his speech was so slow you needed half an hour to listen to the response to a simple, "How ya goin' Barney?"

"Well . . . I'm . . . okay . . . I . . . reckon . . ."

But Barney's speech was as fluent as a river in flood in comparison with that of Kate, his sister.

Kate was so slow that, when propositioned by a travelling salesman, before she could tell him she wasn't a girl like that . . . she was.

Irishman to digger on Anzac Day: "Was it you or your brother that got killed in the war?"

Inmate to another in Long Bay Jail: "Do you want a ticket for the Warden's Ball?"

"Gawd mate," came the reply, "I can't go to a ball in this outfit."

"It's not a dance, mate, it's a raffle."

Why don't Aussie girls wear panties?
To keep the flies off the pies.

The Texan was touring Australia, and found himself in a country pub one Saturday afternoon, telling all and sundry about the size of things back in Texas.

"Why," he said, "back home I can climb in the saddle, and ride all day, and still not reach the other side of the ranch."

"Yeah," said the local, downing his beer, "I know what you mean — I've got a horse like that too."

A truckie stopped in Bourke and asked a local how to get to Cobar.

"Well I certainly wouldn't start from here."

An Aussie's idea of a perfect sight: A Pommie swimming out through Sydney Heads with a New Zealander under each arm.

A man went into his local pub with his dog. Both were in Parramatta colours and both watched the match on TV with avid interest. When Parramatta scored, the dog sat up and yapped excitedly. The new barman watched this performance and finally had to comment on the intelligence of the dog.

"But," he continued, "what does the dog do if the opposing side scores?"

"Somersaults."

"How many?" asked the barman.

"Depends how hard I kick him."

What's the difference between making yoghurt and making an Australian baby?

With yoghurt you have to start with a bit of culture.

Why don't public servants look out of the window in the morning when they go to work?

If they did they wouldn't have anything to do in the afternoons.

The Arab sheik asked each of his three sons what they wanted for Christmas. The oldest wanted a Lear jet, the second a Rolls-Royce, the third, Young Abdul (much younger than the others), wanted a cowboy outfit.

Came Christmas day, the plane and the car were delivered to the tent, but there was no cowboy outfit. The child was very upset.

Time went by and at last a telex arrived saying there was a package on the wharf at Port Said. They took the Rolls-Royce to the port and on the wharf there was a container wrapped in cellophane.

The sheik pulled a gold-plated spanner from his robe and gave it to his son, saying, "Here at last is your cowboy outfit." Young Abdul opened up the container and there inside was the Queensland Cabinet.

Why are Queensland politicians like bananas? They start off green, turn yellow and finally become bent.

Bert was a drover with a wooden eye, the result of losing a battle with a stray from the herd. Bert's wooden eye was painted to match its companion and filled the gap nicely, so to speak. But it made Bert self-conscious and his social life thus suffered. He was sure no woman would want anything to do with him and his wooden eye.

But his friends among the station hands managed finally to persuade him to go to the annual town dance. Nothing, however, would persuade him to ask a girl to dance — until he noticed one not particularly attractive girl sitting out every dance. So he summoned up his courage and sidled up to her.

"I don't suppose," he ventured tentatively, "I don't suppose you'd like a dance?"

"Wouldn' I?" came the reply.

"Well, you're not so perfect yourself!" Bert responded hotly.

Did you hear about the Aussie girl who didn't know she had been raped till the cheque bounced?

Did you hear about the Australian who had a penis transplant?
It didn't take. His hand rejected it.

Of course Australians are decisive people. Doesn't everyone have four national anthems?

Anzac Day. An old digger in the RSL club leant on the bar in a twisted fashion, occasionally putting a beer to his lips in what was obviously a very awkward and painful movement. A reporter doing a story went up to him and said, "Did you get that at Gallipoli, sir?"
"No, Myers. Bastard of a fit, isn't it!"

Glossary

To those of non-Australian persuasion, the following may prove helpful, if not essential, to a better understanding of this tome.

A.I.F. Australian Infantry Force

Anzac Day a day of remembrance for those lost in war. A.N.Z.A.C. is an acronym of Australian and New Zealand Army Corps.

A.S.I.O. Australian Security Intelligence Organisation

backblock sparsely inhabited country

billy an indispensable tin with wire handle, used for cooking on open fires

black stump, beyond the the remotest inland country, the back of beyond

blow hard a person of boastful predisposition

blue heeler a breed of cattle dog

boundary rider a person, in times past a horseman, employed to check and maintain the fences of a property

brekker breakfast, brekkie

bull dust the fine dust that collects in potholes on outback roads

bullocky the driver of a team of bullocks

bung false

bushie an inhabitant of the Australian country or outback or "bush"

chook an adult chicken

chunder, chunderous vomit, and, by extension, as distasteful as vomit

cocky a poor landowner

compo from compensation — a payment received from injuries sustained during work

crook unwell

C.S.I.R.O. Commonwealth Scientific and Industrial Research Organisation

Double Bay an affluent suburb of Sydney

dunny an outside toilet

eatery café

fair dinkum in all truth, straight up

galah a genus of parrot. When preceded by the word flamin', the phrase describes a foolish person.

galoot a flamin' galah (see above)

G'day Good day. The standard salutation

jackaroo an apprentice grazier

kelpie a breed of dog used mainly for working with sheep

Kiwi a New Zealander

kero tin kerosene (paraffin) tin

lamington a square of sponge cake encased in chocolate icing and covered in desiccated coconut

middy a medium-sized glass, usually of beer

Mintie a chewy, mint-flavoured confectionery

mulga the bush or back country, from the species of *Acacia* or mulga found in certain outback areas

Myer's the Australian equivalent of Selfridge's

pommie, pom an Englishman or woman — generally believed to be an acronym of Prisoner of Mother England. The noun is rarely used without the adjectival accompaniment of "whingeing".

ocker, okker 1. the archetypal uncultivated Australian working man
2. a boorish, uncouth, chauvinistic Australian
3. an Australian male displaying qualities considered to be typically Australian, as good humour, helpfulness and resourcefulness. *Macquarie Dictionary*

offsider a helper, friend or partner

rabbiter a person who traps rabbits for profit

redback a small but very poisonous spider

ringer the fastest shearer of a team working together

R.S.L. Returned Servicemen's League

sheila an Australian woman

sickies days taken off work on the pretence of illness

Sinney Sydney, capital of New South Wales

skite a person of boastful predisposition

squatter a rich landowner

Starve the lizards! an exclamation similar to Oh Gosh!

swagman, swaggie an itinerant country worker who carries his possessions in a bundle or swag slung over one shoulder

thongs flip-flops, rubber slip-on sandals

tinny a tin (can) of beer

wharfie a wharf labourer

zinc cream a thick, usually white, sun-protection unguent applied liberally to noses during summer

If your favourite Aussie Joke is missing from this collection and you'd like to see it included in a future edition, please send it to:

Aussie Jokes
Angus & Robertson Publishers
P.O. Box 290
NORTH RYDE NSW 2113

or

Aussie Jokes
Angus & Robertson Publishers
16 Golden Square
LONDON W1R 4BN

A small monetary remuneration and a copy of any revised edition will be forwarded for any new jokes included on publication.